THE PRECARIOUS RHETORIC OF ANGELS

THE PRECARIOUS
RHETORIC OF ANGELS

poems

GEORGE LOONEY

WHITE PINE PRESS   BUFFALO, NEW YORK

The following poems were first published in the journals listed here:

Ascent: "The History of Signification," "An Inside Job," and "Dancing in Miami, Oklahoma." *Gulf Coast:* "Figures We're Meant to Believe In." *Notre Dame Review:* "Faced with a Mosque in a Field of Wheat." *The Evansville Review:* "A Little Water, Served Up with Prayer." *The Bellingham Review:* "The Music of What's Left." *Hayden's Ferry Review:* "Waiting for Clearance." *Black Warrior Review:* "One of Weather's Best Lies." *South Dakota Review:* "Given Time" (under the title "Where Cement Is Cracked"). *New England Review:* "The Blurred Hand Holds More." *Sun Dog:* "Crashes." *Quarterly West:* "Signs Garbled, Incoherent" and "The Precarious Rhetoric of Angels." *Calapooya:* "Soaked to the Skin and Singing." *The Texas Review:* "Flying Northwest over Missouri." *High Plains Literary Review:* "The Coroner's Soliloquy" and "Just Under What We Call Landscape." *The Gettysburg Review:* "Storms That Laugh Bitter and Nostalgic." *Prairie Schooner:* "A Vague Memory of Fish and Sin" (under the title "Fish and Sin"). *Midday Moon:* "Mostly Water, After All" and "Hymns Not One of Us Would Risk." *Alaska Quarterly Review:* "With Enough Heat and a Good Wind" and "Near Aneurysms of Soot." *The Journal:* "So Many Bonfires Out Walking" (under the title "Forecasts of Loneliness and Storms"). *Flyway Literary Review:* "How I Walked with a Woman Across the Maumee." *Passages North:* "A Hosanna for the True Curve of the Body." *Willow Springs:* "The Burning Wheel Put Out by Its Own Turning." *Beloit Poetry Journal:* "We Call It Hot Blood and Hum It." *RUNES 2003:* "Swing Dancing in The Blind Pig." *New Letters:* "The Options of Memory Are Not Infinite." *The Kenyon Review:* "The Sleep of Wood in the Houses of Wrens."

"How I Walked With a Woman Across the Maumee" was selected by Walter McDonald to receive the 1998 *Flyway Literary Review* Award for Poetry.
"The Options of Memory Are Not Infinite" received second runner-up honors in the poetry catagory of the 1998 *New Letters* Literary Awards.
"Crashes," in an earlier version, received honorable mention in The World's Best Short Short Story Competition, 1993.

The White Pine Press Poetry Prize
Volume Number 10

First Edition

10-digit ISBN 1-893-996-42-5
13-digit ISBN 9781893996427

Printed and bound in the United States of America

Library of Congress Control Number: 2005929016

for Douglas, again, &, as always, for my mother

CONTENTS

Between angels, on this earth
absurdly between angels . . .
—Stephen Dunn

Let us first speak of the possible and impossible.
—Aristotle

The History of Signification

First, notice what's missing, how
it insists loss has carved
sandstone and shale, the sad wreck
of language. Between memory
of desire and desire, bodies tend to
remain in motion despite the drag
of gravity. Between presence
and the grief of signifiers, no
two syllables add up to anything.
Next, give up on absence, and focus
on a surface that can still
surprise you, stubborn, caught
between states, both memory
and the insistence of
a moment. Gravity is continuous.

Rocks in Arizona have been
carved into forms that signify
nothing. Loss is
elitist and forgetting is best
done in layers. Something
as continuous as gravity isn't
humbled by the long collapse
of rock into soil. Water is
amnesic. The distance between
what things were and what they are
sifts through fingers. Between
what is said and what is,
don't forget that, at its best, flesh
signifies. Meaning
alludes to something lost. All

the details in the world don't
add up. Between things,
hover for years before falling
toward whatever bends the world
around it until it is
the world. Pray for memory
to be what's remembered. The distance
between the two illumines cliffs
with pictographs, the history of
signification, a story of loss
that would paint everything in
colors ground from rock. No theory
makes grief intelligible,
or replaces what's missing
with more than the gravity of loss.

Figures We're Meant to Believe In

Coal runs veins under what was
never clarity. *Just missing,*
a miner might have said of his wife,
come home to a crevice
and vague dust. His wife had been
asleep in the house. Now,
every corpse carried out of the earth
has her face. Or she's behind him wanting
to hear what he can't say,
his heart collapsing in his chest.
This miner is invention, but the crevice
and a roof pleated by pressure
are real. And hearts can be
exhausted and years later collapse,
like the vein that swallowed
the miner's house, his wife, trapped
inside, becoming, with time,
a sad replica of a saint or demon
carved from stone and bolted down
in a cathedral to balance the remarkable
light passing through figures
we're meant to believe in. It is stone
we put our faith in and build on.
Miners, like monks, must listen to hearts
echoing dust and not doubt
the stability of the world. Love,
they say, follows a vein in the heart
until it's tapped out, every beat
a collapse, dust, falling
through the body, a reminder
faith needs air. Nothing connects us
to the earth more than lungs.

This, both miners and monks
say, is no abstraction.

FACED WITH A MOSQUE IN A FIELD OF WHEAT

The hint of moraines on the horizon
argues against certainty. Unlike
the ruins of the shoe factory,
where it's said ghosts murmur and often cry,
barefoot and sore, glaciers are in it
for the long haul. Rust, though,
just hangs around and starts rumors
of couples laying blankets down
over ruins, touching each other
into moans. Not even sex
can disguise the flatness of a place
topographical maps turn gray
and the sky blurs, anonymous.
Any vague history of loss is oral.
Everything depends on the sad, moving tongue
and the safe lies of memory,
the past a ventriloquist, a mosque
gone gray surrounded by wheat. Autumn,
the fields on fire turning everything
to smoke, the mosque blurs into
a definition of what the heart gives up
to live in the flesh, a fervent prayer
faith makes things come back. It's said

glaciers will come south again
and erase scars from the last time.
That's just rumor. Nothing's certain
but the hacking of Sufis in the minarets,
smoke from their lungs
a kind of confession. It is
the world that's burning they love,
chants they cough through

elegies for everything consumed.
They don't know the history of ice and faith
and loss this landscape is
the text of. What they believe
is the world is formed by rusty voices
singing among ruins, that
any voice drifting with the ash of
the right crop can save everything,
that cars hurtling down the state route
are driven by dummies
they can throw their scarred voices into
and speak of sex and the anonymous sky.
Smoke can't hold up a mosque.
Local myths tell of feet pulled loose
by hooks in the river. It's said

the feet flatten wheat into what might be
topographical maps of distant countries
where the heart's had too much wine,
where ruins are stone and the ice
never reached. *This heart's a foreigner
everywhere*, a drunk says, faced
with a mosque in a field of wheat.
From the minarets, Sufis read maps
flattened in crops by wind or feet,
the sky a chant in the bitter language of rust
or fire thrown into the throats
of lovers moaning in the ruins of a factory.
Ash isn't all burning leaves.
Glaciers are breaking off, moving south
like ghosts of feet. It's said
when they get here history will buckle

under its guilt and religion
will lose its voice, gone hoarse
denying the world. For now,
farmers burn their fields to clear off
what hands can't, and Sufis
translate the smoke
into one of many voices, unheard.

A Little Water, Served Up with Prayer

An armadillo snuffles and burrows in
the dust behind dying bushes
strung with brittle remnants of flowers,
their centers hysterical crosses.
Just south, its mate dries out. Here,
everyone wishes water back.

Some believe the world is in dire need
of cleansing. Dust
convinces them a little water,
served up with prayer,
is all that's needed. The sweet flesh
still moist in the shell of

the armadillo is the color of
drenched streets in some distant city
where gospel music soaks the air
around the clock, whether
or not anyone listens. A local station
is fed programming from there.

Some hear it without radios,
recognizing its rhythms in the dust.
Baptism, they say, is the only cure.
Children peel the brittle skin
of fathers asleep in front of TVs
where preachers blame the weather

on the sins of men and women.
One daughter swallows the skin
and prays Forgiveness,
her name for the armadillo,

makes it safe across the roads
to the shrunken pond

without finding its mate. Her father's
dry flesh tastes like a hymn
she's heard every Sunday morning
she remembers. Nothing,
not even this drought, can convince her
to uncurl her heart and expose

its belly a knife could write in easy.
No inscribed prayer will sway her.
Not even her father's flesh,
swallowed, will call her heart out
of its shell to compose hymns
to echo in her like cathedrals.

The Music of What's Left

The murmurous haunt of flies on summer eves.
—John Keats

Sad, to think of the murmurous haunt
of flies Keats spoke of
lost to the vagaries of genetics.

Not even the church—with its ash
and incense, its sin
and liturgies—can revive the lost song

of eighteenth century flies.
All stories told well
end in flies, or the flat murmur

of what isn't a heart but wind
in the architecture
of some cathedral burned,

sold, and renovated into a restaurant
where a man was murdered
who only wanted the Orange Roughy,

Cajun style. Ruin hums under
any ritual, and witnesses
disagree about the odd flash

one diner thought was evidence
of someone's birthday.
No one noticed the thin gauze

of dust drifting down from
what had once been
the cross-vault of a church set fire to

by a woman mad from the vagaries
of love. Now, the story,
once so clear-cut by lead bezels

into figures who would have cursed
the necessity of flies,
forgets itself, and the flies,

and focuses, sad, on how the bullet
sanctified the heart
it passed through. No fault of

its own, the coroner says later, drunk
and weary, into a mike.
This heart was sound, no sign

of a murmur or scar tissue. No damage
at all, except for
the cauterized tunnel. Bad design,

how knocking down one wall
compromises the whole structure,
makes it unlivable, open to flies.

After the fact, witnesses,
and those not there, tend to talk
about warning signs. In this story,

they say the woman stared too cruel
at her fish. All the flies
since Keats hum the music

of what's left. Sad, how a face
can end up collapsed
on a fish, blackened. How old women

light candles in churches and listen
for the infinitesimal
hum of another world. Sad,

how choirs sing in the heat
and swat flies on Sundays,
the world insisting it is always

with us. *It wasn't the fish*
that killed him, but love,
the chef says. And the saints,

who saw it all, would nod
in their traps of lead and color,
if lead and glass could nod.

It's all about judgment. Sad,
to think it comes down
to the work of flies erasing the proof

bodies would leave. Sad,
how everyone danced ballroom style,
the woman taken out in handcuffs

ranting about cross-beams
and his heart, its
baroque architecture. Singing,

we slap each other's backs and laugh,
imagining elaborate tunnels
through which we might, one day,

escape, Keats' flies, nothing like
angels, come to show us, for
better or worse, the easy way out.

WAITING FOR CLEARANCE

Water's gone poison in these narrow ditches
that separate the highway and the dying
fields. Cows sniff, back off, not thirsty enough
to dip their long faces into such distance.

Memory is a town that seems to float, broken,
along the horizon. You could be drinking
in a bar in that town, where pain has circled
the airfield for years, waiting for clearance.

An old widower lived at the far end of one
of the landing strips. Cows used to wander
into his sleep, ghosts whose hot tongues
scraped his skin, his heart echoing the vague

rhythms of flight. He closed the bar every night,
haunted by the constant circling of curses
half-uttered. Loss stumbled along with him,
too drunk to utter more than the ghostly low

of a cow tipped over in some fallow field
even the moon had abandoned. Curses
can't bring down towns or flood rivers.
No town without an airport offers more for pain

than drink. You would pull Loss gently from
a ditch and dry it out enough to hold it
and whisper a name in its ear it could believe.
Pain lumbers through the cows cursed

with what ghosts carved in their skin and forgot.
The buzzing they hear could be insects,
or a disgruntled ghost cursing the desire
language has for meaning. Whatever starves

under the bruised sky haunts us,
memory not tipped over. And abandoned
towers still bring ghosts in safe, clearance
a word you wouldn't think to trade for love.

An Inside Job

All this fuss about the ethereal.
Even the rock everything's built on
will give in to dust. Plates of it
shift under our feet, enough friction
to make bones sing like angels
who've lost the only map to the flesh.
Under us, heat is signing a lease
and moving in, its possessions
prone to breakage and speaking

in tongues, loss the music
it plays to seduce. Our lovers
stare with mute longing
past hardwood floors and hum
slow melodies of heat and erosion.
Last night, down the block,
someone broke in to a house
affluent in linoleum. Flour
was busted, bags of it,

and the white replicas of hands
in a dance of touch wouldn't
give away anything. Identity is
such a tricky disguise. Officials
go from house to house after hands
damned and bleached by dust.
No one expects to find anything.
The heat's rising out of the rock,
cajoling our bones, coaxing them

to think about abandoning
the burden of flesh. Landscape is
an obvious disguise. We want
to know what was taken,
and what bodies were tectonic
while it happened, to know
if touch can leave us and dust
the world as if to say *something*
has to last. The details will

come out slow in the press.
An inside job, we'll learn. We have
a criminal who's local and knows
the famous flatness here
is deceptive, every story it tells
weak on motive, the language
what keeps us reading,
the bitter, worn moraines
elegies for everything taken.

One of Weather's Best Lies

In fog these silos, backlit by the mall,
become a cathedral. Earlier,
a train made a graven image out of
a stalled car, the gargoyles
on this cathedral laughing, or shaking,
come down with a virus. Carved of
local limestone, they cringe in
low clouds. *If weather were a woman*
fog would be better at lies, a drunk says,
gargoyles clawing their hearts,
wives drinking cheap wine and chanting
the names of stone over snoring men.

This drunk has coughed up sour blood
and ranted at love and weather enough
he's local legend. In a few days,
folks will sit, sober, in stale pews,
and the sorrow of stained glass
will turn the bruises of women,
disguised by base, into faint blossoms
in the fragile light. Weather
has nothing on people. If it were clear,
these silos would lie
about how easy the past is to sift.
Everything goes bad given time.

Even the mall will rant its way to ruin,
lights abandoning the flickering halos
of bugs, shops as empty
as the woman the drunk loved
who couldn't love anyone less scarred.
Foreign words tattooed on her chest

forgave everyone who loved her
but the drunk. She wasn't
an angel, despite the wings burned on her
back, and not even an angel
can forgive battered landscapes,
or the whiskey the drunk mistakes
for a blessing. If I knelt in this
ghost cathedral, no prayer would come.

Curses turn mouths to stone.
Six miles to the south, men blast dust
out of gouges in landscape,
and cough blossoms of shale and limestone.
Weather delivers the dust north
for miles—here, in fog, a dance
for gravity's sake. Faith keeps
the drunk ranting at the funeral,
cursing false angels, cathedrals
of air and dust, and dances
that lie. *Whiskey and weather aren't accidents,*
he says. The silos, full of a slow drifting down
and enough heat, might burn
and char the sky, and make me
face the wreckage of a car
that burns and isn't consumed.

The drunk has said fog is the voice of
the woman he loved. Tonight,
it rants, a virus that leaves me burning up
and looking to the sky
to salve a heart. It's one of weather's
best lies, that storms heal

with enough sacrifice. Tonight,
I could give up this cathedral
and drink secular wine
with a woman who's never heard Latin,
the sky clear for miles.
Without a cathedral, men, drunk in bars
to the south, cough and rant,
until closing, about saints and bruises.
Here, fog's a curse, my knees dust.

GIVEN TIME

A woman buries cantaloupe and corn
in the broken brick yard
where trains used to stop for poker and beer
and women whose throats
erupted in song. Such decay
will feed roots enough, she thinks,
to turn this into pasture,

bricks giving in to dust. Maybe
she thinks burial's still necessary
for resurrection, that
a train's trembling in the earth
is just the hint melons need.
Corn knows enough without the help,
burying them together

a hedge against misunderstandings.
Nothing gives full-throated women
as much pleasure as believing
that, given time, cantaloupes
will burst through where bricks
are cracked in patterns that suggest stories
of country waltzes they'd love

to sing to men until their cards went blank
and their beer flat, until
not even trains would remember to stop.
Here, women leave men rotting in beds
and sing of despair
in abandoned brick yards, faith
the only thing that keeps the earth going.

THE BLURRED HAND HOLDS MORE

for Joanna

No doubt you've heard of the silo diver.
They say he times it
so the wheat bends south
in what wind there is
before falling in some semblance
of grace. No one can say
why he's never hurt. His skin,
pale, barely covers his veins
and glares over the wheat
that seems to reject him.
It's the direction of the wheat,
he says, it has to be
falling away. Not even wheat
breaks under him His bones
should be a doctrine of desolate cracks
in the humming light
of the X-ray wall,
but they're as white and clear
as the Elvis painted
on the silo's side, a study in white
on white. It's the Vegas Elvis,
and the knuckles blur
where he clutches the mike,
as if the painter had to drink
in order to get it right,
and failed from too much bourbon.
It's a delicate balance.
So is his body and the wheat.
Any mistake and it's over.
Elvis didn't sing from his throat.
The voice came up coughing and raw

from being held under
the foul surface of the Tennessee swamp
that was all he had left
to call a heart in Vegas.
The silo diver whispers *Love me tender*
as he falls toward the wheat.
Maybe wheat can listen,
or maybe wind loves his bright body
falling through it, a song.
Locals say the Elvis of the silo
saves him, believing
the blurred hand holds more than a mike.
Tomorrow a crowd will gather
for his dive, the sky as gray
as Ohio gets. The diver's sore heart
will forget the wheat.
He'll dive for a woman
behind the fanatics who swear Jesus
smiles in blurred knuckles.
Not even Elvis will save him this time.

CRASHES

Manuel straps families into cars
he knows will collide
with cement walls. He makes sure

all the buckles are fastened
and looks in their faces, believing
they know what's coming.

His wife can't understand his guilt.
They're dummies, she whispers in his ear
after love. She sings to him

in the language of the country
his father dreamed of till he died,
and strokes his chest. Still,

cars pass through his dreams and smash
against the night. One evening
Manuel passes an accident,

police pulling bloodied bodies out.
He doesn't recognize this,
nothing familiar. Later,

he can't touch his wife in bed.
Even the sheets around his flesh
make him ill, his sleep

a boy thrown through a windshield
all night. The next day,
Manuel ignores the whispers

and kisses the children,
holding the hand of the mother.
His dreams are full of crashes.

One night, he almost turns
to his wife, a wooden
boy shattering in his chest.

SIGNS GARBLED, INCOHERENT

The sheriff tells the press the body shows no signs
of abuse, and the sweet scent she gives off isn't
explainable. A mute shepherd found the girl naked in bushes

and ran into town signing, his hands stuttering down
Main. Tonight, while the mute shepherd gets drunk,
the sheriff notices the sweet scent the girl gives off

seeps all over town. Tomorrow, his wife complains
at her deli about his hands, how, when he touched her
last night, she couldn't feel them. She tells a regular

where he touched her her body went numb. She wraps
the salmon and says it must be the girl, that sweetness.
It's unnatural, she says, *and getting worse.* The girl's

sweet-smelling body ignores them all. Someone sees
the sheriff walking down a back street, his hands
a blur in the dark, almost an unfinished notion

of hands. *The whole town stinks of her sweetness,*
the bartender tells the mute shepherd, making another
rum and Coke. Down the bar, a deaf woman is drunk,

her signing garbled, incoherent. The mute shepherd
can't make out a thing. The sheriff's wife closes the deli
and walks to the edge of town, to the quarry where

her last customer said she had seen her husband, sitting
on a rock, singing what sounded, from a safe distance,
like hymns. Out here, the sweetness is almost bearable.

She's surprised at first by the sheep milling about, crying,
but then remembers the rumors of the drunk shepherd,
the one who found the girl. The sheep must be looking for

him. From where she is she can see what's left of her
husband's hands moving as if he were giving directions.
But what his almost-hands sign in the air over the sheep

is not a map of town, not the way to get to the bar where
the mute shepherd helps the deaf drunk out the door.
It's her body he signs to the abandoned sheep. She has

never been so uncertain what sweetness is. Her husband
reproduces every curve and imperfection of her body,
every subtle inflection. It is the most amazing thing

she has seen, her body drawn so sweetly by the blurs of
her husband's hands. The sheep head into town. Already
she hears doors slamming as people come out to see what is

happening, the bitter smell of the sheep cleansing the town
of the girl's unbearable sweetness. The sheriff is crying.
His wife goes to him and places his hands, which are hands

again, on her body. The shepherd leads the sheep out of town
and sings songs about women and pain and forgiveness.
No one is left awake to hear him and marvel. The sweetness

dissipates until only the girl smells so sweet. *It's not for
the living,* the bartender says to the deaf drunk at the end
of the bar again, *that sweetness. It's more than we can bear.*

The deaf drunk takes another drink and winks at the bartender.
Though she's never heard a word he's said, his voice
trembles across her flesh, the touch a sweetness she needs.

Soaked to the Skin and Singing

Maps tell nothing of how towns got where
they are, nothing of rumor
and the local myths of women dancing
to juke boxes in murky bars,
the men they go home with folded up,
faded. Lines aren't always roads
named and paved, and north,
on a body, is often a lie. Following
flesh can lose anyone, some
lines obscure dirt roads no one names.
Shacks hum a chorus of weeds
where they end. A drunk
who calls one home started drinking
the day a lizard bit his wife's chest.

Touch was amphibious after that,
and cold blooded. Whiskey
flicked his throat raw. His wife
would yell for him to touch her.
Heal me, she'd beg. The lizard had
sunk one tooth in each breast. *Stigmata*,
the drunk swore. Her body hissed,
a landscape that steamed and sank
under shacks. Not even Christ
can save those buried by being
swallowed. There was no ground
that was safe. No map to show
where the next touch would go under,
nothing but rumor below her skin.

Alone, he stumbled down streets named
for the memory of the roiling
of fish. After a downpour,
he'd be soaked to the skin and singing.
Rumor kept him believing no map
had everything right. He'd lost
the faith it takes to touch a body
into a map with all roads
clearly drawn. With enough faith
he might have named every road,
even the ones with bridges that sway
in high winds to sad songs
women pay for to dance
with anonymous men in sinking bars.

FLYING NORTHWEST OVER MISSOURI

for William Trowbridge, and for Kong

Turbulence was expected. Even air wants
notice. A woman, caressed by her lover
from lift-off to this, the descent, bends over
and loses it. Sorry, the pilot says
for weather. But even on the ground,
we've always known weather was a gamble.
This woman, her lover's hand holding her
hair back, speaks for those of us afraid to
let it out, as they say. The world miniature
and real does that. Air shattering, dropping us
hundreds of feet in seconds, makes amnesia
something to wish for. Our regaining altitude,
as blessings go, no better than a mixed one.

This vague Antarctic of clouds could be where
Mary Shelley's creature walked off with a chip
on his shoulder the size of an afterlife,
or maybe just the size of this undignified wasp
of forlorn metal that casts its shadow over
what could be the creature's footprints. Far off,
caves are flutes for wind the engines keep us from
hearing, moaning fugues about how much loss
vengeance has to swallow. It comes to me
the creature couldn't die, that he realized this,
and put on a gray suit and financed movies
when no one else believed in the future
of those sad and flickering figures of light.

For years, he was behind movies where the lost
jerk through grainy landscapes toward women
they love. Finally, he put all he had left

into a movie where he remade himself in the guise
of an ape big enough in black and white stop-action
to act out his rage and then fall to its end
while a pale woman, who remembered the feel
of the huge palm under her like a bed, sobbed
in the puny arms of a man who'd never
be enough. To lose a world, like Kong did,
to have it ripped from you by a woman
or some blind man's son, requires the creation
of a new vocabulary where the heart is

large enough for a man to live in, each
chamber an obscure definition of absence,
a longing to be filled with salt and sound.
The creature would have nothing to do with
the remake, the grace of the special effects
too forgiving. In fact, he wanted to lose it
at the gala premiere, but the tux was rented
and the girl who sold him popcorn smiled.
There are moments, he knows, too perfect
to ruin. The way the lover of the woman
turbulence got to could be said to define
the grace even a normal heart can manage,
weather permitting. Every bit of science in

the world can't predict something as simple
as how any of our bodies will respond
to the vagaries of air or the blinding curse
of clouds. And not even the creature could have
guessed how far his ape would go, or how many
women would lose it and cry in the quiet
dark of movie houses when the giant lungs

gave up. Some falls no one survives, not even
a myth. The original Kong didn't have
computer-generation to make us feel
sorry for him, and didn't ask us to walk
in his shoes. He was just Kong, and we knew
what to expect with him. Finally descending

under the clouds to land, I want to revise
the ending. I want there to be enough air
to lower that great ape-god with a grace
usually reserved for small things like feathers
or hair, the hair a woman's lover holds back
from her face to kiss her as she straddles him
in the bed they fall into after surviving
the turbulence in clouds haunted by the shunned
and abandoned, where storms could've been
a language that recovers what we've lost
or discarded. Back on the ground, we risk
weather all the time, sure what we might lose
down here isn't something we can't live without.

The Coroner's Soliloquy

It's about what's left. Fragments, like this one,
they find in fields and bring me. Tell us,
they say, who killed her and how. They know
a little, enough to recognize
the femur of a woman, how it locks
into the pelvic joint, but they don't
know what this says about the victim.
Sometimes, one comes to me whole,
uncorrupted. They wheel the body in
and leave, done with it, the necessary
opening something they can't imagine,
more delicate than they think. It is
a ritual, opening flesh. Actually,
the fear of intimacy turns them away.
I know how they whisper, how they joke,
nervous. They can't admit they envy
how I tender to these bodies
their last remnants of love, which is, after all,
only a question of attention paid.
The field where they found this one is being
dug up. They tell me they hope to find more.
Here, I'd like to tell them, is more
than enough. This, I'd say, is no woman,
but a myth made carnate. This is what's left.

STORMS THAT LAUGH BITTER AND NOSTALGIC

Truth is, what was found in the desert
outside Roswell is lost.
The last to admit seeing something
has Alzheimer's, but says it
wasn't dummies or weather balloons.
Not even his wife believed,
and left cursing him and his faith.
Sometimes he forgets, and imagines
the photographs of a woman
in every room are from an autopsy.
Aliens are angels, he says. They drink
the whiskey and the gin
his wife left. When storms refuse to
settle, he stays up and translates
anonymous patterns in the dust
on end tables—strange circles
he thinks are alien maps
drawn to a scale only heaven knows.
Doctors have explained what's going on
in his head, but he thinks of
the illness as a storm
that flattens crops into the figures
of angels, or fish swollen
and rotting. He believes storms
hide more than stars. He wants to
visit ponds high up in the mountains
where fish blur the water
with their bodies and the dust
they kick up. From overhead,
the water looks like a map
of the state where his wife is
forgetting him. Mannequins

in Roswell's mall wear next to
nothing. They have his
wife's sad face, and strange designs
carved in their bellies or backsides,
tattoos almost. He knows
what they mean. Truth is,
dust has told him stories for years
of abduction and sacrilege.
No one's coming back. The whiskey
has gone bitter, and the gin
is just gone. So much is lost,
it hurts to remember. In Roswell,
men drink and circle statues downtown,
cursing women who've headed off
to real places like Albuquerque.
All the mannequins in the mall
whisper in his wife's sober voice.
What's never photographed
is, in the end, what's believed.

Dying Slow and Loved in Massillon, Ohio

Water runs hysterical here, and crude,
through a landscape with scars
local stories explain. The drunk who curses
blurs everything, even the woman
whose touch you believed could heal any hurt.
When he's cut off and rants out the door,
follow him. To witness his collapse
will let you read your own scars like a map.
Whether or not this river foams

with what could be bruises or carp,
calm water's false. Trusting it leads to drink,
a heart enlarged and damned.
Dahlias, lashed together under umbrellas
at the edge of town, are protected from sun
and rain that would blur their petals
to ruin. Nothing's allowed to touch them
until some false color trickles in.
Then, locals vie for the chance to cart off

armfuls to die slow and loved inside
their homes. North, whiskey bottles tossed
miles back curse what current's left,
water blurred and run down. The field
where the drunk collapses and you hold him
is the crude rant of weeds. But dahlias,
enough of them, could forgive everything.
Maybe every scar, real or imagined,
longs for an armful of imperfect dahlias.

THE SEA HAS MOVED SOUTH

The old neighborhood is being upscaled,
dry-lipped strangers said. You can stay,
they told the sea, but the moon, well,
the moon is definitely out. They said
something about him being two-faced, how
he pulls at the bodies of total strangers.
Too promiscuous for the family feel
they wanted. Too indiscriminate, they said.
The moon is a poser, pretending to be
light. They said the sea's role would have
to be diminished. Relying too much on
anything, they said, makes people more
prone to sin. The sea grimaced and took
their money, bought an old house
in a different neighborhood. Some nights
the sea sits out on the porch and drinks
fuzzy navels she mixes in mason jars.

Tonight, the moon came knocking, and knocked
until his knuckles bled before he left,
cursing the sea and change. The sea had
had too many navels and blacked out,
and missed the moon's last offer to take her
away from all this. The moon is
the big loser here. The sea has a house
with a wrap-around porch, schnapps, and a maid
twice a week. All the moon has is what he has
lost. The moon has been dumped before.
Scars pock-mark his face and people name them,
even call some seas. Tomorrow, the sea
will wake in her own bed with no memory
of how she got there, the sheets, rumpled,

forming the map of a face, one with long rifts
the sea will want to sink into, drawn to
something so familiar it doesn't need a name.

A Vague Memory of Fish and Sin

Some rivers bend from sight or burn down
to nothing but fossils and dust.
With this kind of loss, it's hard
to lay blame. My mother used to say
we were tied to water. Even Jesus,
she said, fed the multitudes with fish,
and called Peter a fisher of men.

Every Friday, I was too scared to eat,
sure stigmata would blossom from the sole
she served with a tartar sauce
with lemon that would scorch my mouth
and turn it into the cave where an ex-priest
ate the bones of fish he caught to atone
for the desperate sins he imagined

when in the parish he was the star of
every confession he heard. I'd hide
the fish in napkins, stock up on potatoes
and green beans, and excuse myself
after dessert to slip the accursed fish
into the compost where strays fed.
Even now, the thought of fish is enough

to make me cringe and believe I must not
be saved. Nothing nets bring out of water
can bless this world where rivers die
and what's left in water's absence could be
dull salt and the despair of insects.
Deep in the compost, larvae hatched
and burrowed towards a vague memory

of fish stink and sin. Adult by
the time they broke through decay to the air,
they followed what was left of a dying river
and fed swallows for miles. Or
ended up in the carcasses of fish
too small to be kept. Fishing is an art,
and a pleasure. But it's hard to believe

pleasure is all it's cracked up to be,
or even close to enough to comfort
the priest who cracked under the pressure
of all that flesh that kept begging
for absolution. I'd like to find the cave
with what's left of that penitent confessor,
tell his bones the color of salt everything.

MOSTLY WATER, AFTER ALL

This river needs rain. The fish taste too much
like desperation, all the butter and garlic in
the world not enough to make them edible.
Today, a bitter woman will dive off the bridge.
Some boys will find her buried in mud to her hips.
Dared, they'll touch her legs and stare between them.
Later, the coroner will cite semen and bruises
along her thighs and inside her as evidence
of foul play. When they find the suspect in a bar,
a domestic beer glazing his hand damp, he'll swear,

sad, he hasn't touched anyone in years.
The bartender will nod, and believe nothing
good has ever come of love. The river will
seem nervous, boys skipping stones across it
and whispering about the body. Guilt isn't
an issue. We might as well blame the drought.
We're mostly water, after all. The suspect
won't be a match, and be let go. The beer
will taste bitter but do what he needs it to.
He'll stumble home, dream the arc of her dive

outlined a bridge over a river of sand,
its weathered wood inscribed with sentences,
grammar not an issue for the writer,
fragments common, nothing making sense.
A woman will claw out of the sand. Naked,
her skin will glisten and she will come to him
and whisper the wood's sentences in his ear.
When she touches him, boys down river
will be skipping stones across sand the bartender
will be clawing his way into, whimpering.

With Enough Heat and a Good Wind

Water's a vague ghost here, the rumor
of an urge to rise. Flatness
does that. Just out of town, a man
rents hot air balloons that gasp
over filled-in swamp. Men and women
point them out to children and each other
when they hear the heavy breath
in clouded skies. Warm air can lift us,

but simply rising is no way out.
I could gasp my way from here to the river
miles south of town and not convince
anyone to wave. Drifting above it,
landscape becomes someone's unfinished joke,
and perspective's just a lie to cover
distances. Water in its best form carves
its own elegy in shale or whatever mineral

is local. Men die in blasts for granite
or limestone, or live to cough themselves
to an early grave. Their breath
condemned by dust, this coughing
is the closest they come to release.
Women stay up late and listen to
the gasps of men with hearing gone bad
and hands that tremble dust. Asleep,

they dream of rivers cresting well past
flood stage, cleansing the world. Of pain,
these women say it's nothing.
What gets to them is how the damn balloons
hover like curses over their flat homes.

Some days it seems if they breathed right
they could drift up from the dust and flood
their bitter lungs with an air clean enough

to be called forgiveness. Even their babies
point to the balloons. And dreams
more and more find dreamers gasping
over their lives, wind the only voice
they recognize. The Black Swamp, rising,
floods basements in homes south of town.
Ruined couches and end tables rot in backyards
where children sew cotton rags together

to make balloons. With enough heat
and a good wind, they believe,
nowhere is too far to reach. Leakage
isn't a stranger. They're not concerned.
Air is always coming and going.
They just want enough distance
to let the explosions in rock
be jokes. Fathers nod off in front of

televisions with their stale shows about
local history. The children hum,
sewing on floors colored by flickering light,
staying up late enough to learn off the TV
what ghosts are. Some learn numbers
to die for, calling women who whisper
love. Some dream of drifting over their homes
in ragged balloons they've sewn themselves.

Dark and Light at Odds

Vern says Melinda yelled from a block away.
Two houses down, a woman said something
to a screen door he swears sounded like *Believe
in hymns and sin.* Vern knows sin
and remembers hymns and hard pews, his mother
shuffling to the altar to receive. The choir
would sing some hymn while the congregation
took in the body and blood. He believed
one girl, singing, was an angel. Her left eye
wandered and he would try to let his own go,
wanting to see like her, though he worried
such vision might drive angels mad. Melinda,
he says, couldn't see past what he couldn't do
for her. In bed, she wouldn't open her eyes.
Vern says it scared him, the thought of her seeing
darkness so well with him inside her.
I want to say she's no good, but can't
come straight out and lie to Vern. And Melinda
is good, I know. As Vern tells it,
when she's through with him every night
his hog-tied carcass hangs upside down
from an oak, his heart slipped down his throat
to whisper a crazed morse code in his sore mouth
until it's a music his feet would dance to,
if not for the rope binding his raw ankles.
Of course, that's not how Vern puts it.
He just says, *She's got her claws in my heart.*
The rest is me. Vern does say Melinda's eyes
love the dark. Anonymous sex, for her,
a hymn without lyrics. He says it could be
he's got everything wrong. Could be the girl
with the loose eye still sings in some church,

her angelic voice and her eye making boys
shudder to feel their hearts clicking on.
Vern's been sitting in the dark working on his own
eye. Almost has it to where he can let it go,
he says, almost to where he can see how
Melinda and the girl in the choir are angels,
dark and light at odds. How love is
finding the one eye that can't let you go.

Determined Planar Foldings

It's not enough to admit things
are getting worse. A woman
fills my apartment with copies
her out-of-state mother sends,
charged to the monks she works for
and often graces with origami
that hunker in the centers of tables.
The copies advise acknowledgment and fade
into a gray confession. But admission

has no more significance to me
than any other racket. All that rots
in the body has a voice.
I could say the copies
are tapestries, complex weavings
of form and language, the design
itself the flaw. That is
the meat of it, isn't it, that the body is
flawed? Though to say paper animals

formed by determined planar foldings
indicate things are getting worse,
this may be only a gesture. Disease is
often related to what leaves us
through our porous flesh. In the case
of my fluids, it's sugar
telling parables of rot. The daughter of
the woman who indulges in origami
insists knowledge is a folding of planes

to form landscapes and figures who whisper
blessings. Monks, they are, the kind
who raise dogs and brew ale. Maybe
this woman's right. That is
the thought I'd fold in paper
and form into vague hints of the ideal
of the figure no figure ever was.
Maybe all this origami is a way
to speak of our bodies, not as *flawed,*

but as *flaws.* Maybe what would be
enough is not the issue. Maybe
monks are right to hold booze
between their legs and cough dust
their trucks kick up in circles
just out of sight of the monastery,
the hills around them slanted, collapsing
like some disease of the blood.
Maybe drunken praise is the same

as drunken curses, and neither
could fold anything out of poisoned air
anyone could live on. Maybe
I should slick myself up, put on a cassock
brown and crusted with the sweet
drippings of a holy body, and drive
to where a woman folds menageries.
Maybe I should join the monks
she cares for, and keep any confession

in hunkering silence, her daughter
sending me letter after letter
I'd fold into rough caricatures
of animals that could be failures
of some god, waiting for
their hearts to take up the spaces
where bodies given to denial are
going to rot. Maybe the future,
with or without admission, isn't enough.

NEAR ANEURYSMS OF SOOT

Down here, where the carcasses of cows
feed an amnesia of flies,
water's a curse that rots out inscriptions
only the dead can decipher.
Cliffs sizzle with the longing of flies.
What river's left has no prayer,
having written promises in rock
it can't keep. Blocked off
with bovine corpses, it curses
the stubbornness of flesh and memory
is an eroded hieroglyph. Decay
takes time. To forget birds
drawn on papyrus or shale mean something
is easy to do. What's lost isn't
so much a prayer as a whispered plea
a lover would have to honor,
or take off shoes and socks and wade into
what's left of a river at the feeble end
of a canyon not even the dead
can hear the past in, their faded chants
what must be inscribed on cave walls
near aneurysms of soot.
No one can translate what the river says.
Not even the dead, who, if asked,
would swear it is nonsense. And true
lovers don't need canyons,
or blood, or the carcasses of cows
blocking a river to a slow trickle,
not enough left to wade in
or cross a cursed forehead with.
As if giving water a shape
a body could be draped on

could absolve the bitter end
of this dying river, or bless
every human mark made on rock.

So Many Bonfires Out Walking

This window hurts with sun, the glare.
Skies that have ranted, and rant,
through its glass and dust
won't forgive how I want to remember

everything wrong. Not cleaned
for years, little gets through
other than a ghost mumbling for whiskey.
Beer won't do it. What he's been through

needs something hard enough to
make any light an excuse
to forget a woman's lips forming
his name. Something hard enough

to burn even bone to ash. It's not
dumb luck bodies are out burning
in this light. Not even whiskey's enough.
The ghost is mine to clean up

or curse, loss the name of the dance
dust does in the afternoon light
in a room where someone sleeps
and slurs the name of this

forgetful ghost, someone who has
written names in lazy dust.
Anything written in dust is
about loss. Storms can shatter glass

but not the indifference of a woman.
Maybe her name was Rachel. It was
something biblical. This is
about how bodies burn in the right light.

So many bonfires out walking,
they could almost forgive everyone.
They do, if Rachel's the right name.
But forgiveness is a lie. On days like this,

the glare off windows blinds everyone,
and clouds lie down in cornfields
to burn with light or absolution. I want
touch to be possible for bodies

of light. I want to believe burning
doesn't have to consume what it burns,
that dust waltzing breath is sanctified
by the whispered name. Rachel,

forgive every ghost, every drunk. Love
how no curse burns us down
to indifference. Love whiskey enough
to kill the bottle and hold someone for luck.

How I Walked with a Woman Across the Maumee

Dream a sad river, if you have to. Dream
a plain white sign with lines and numbers
to show how far the river's forgotten
itself. Make the river the Maumee. Say
it's low from drought, and poison. Drink it
in the diner's coffee just off the highway
where the waitress is friendly but tired,
her second shift in a row. She slips out of
her shoes without shame when you offer to
rub her feet for a meal. Not even this

could forgive how I walked with a woman
across the Maumee on rocks that longed
for any current, how we laughed standing
where the river had been, a long drought
letting us stand there and laugh. I could
rub the sore feet of every waitress
in every faded diner the length of this river
and only scratch my penance. Even lips
to calloused flesh wouldn't be enough. Being
tender is a beginning, with no end

in sight. I caressed a sad woman once
in the absence of a river, wanting
only to know the various textures
of flesh, my fingers tributaries of
a river I'm still learning is more fragile
than any raw water of fish and force
that swells and disappears with weather.
Touching a woman is the closest I'll come
to any kind of forgiveness. *Not enough,*
the recovered Maumee chants when I drive

the state route that follows it with a longing
a bruised waitress, her feet going numb
in a man's hands, could explain. If she could
remember a man with dust for hands
who touched her body until *it* was dust
and a car going by on the broken road,
close enough to be more than sound, lifting her
in its wake, I'd believe the past
has nothing to do with dust or rivers.
That it's a weathered sign remembering

a building burned down where people once ate
in the center of town, two charred bodies
found embracing in the ruin of ash
and smoke. Everyone recognized Rachel,
the woman who'd worked there so long
her name was coffee in the bitter mouth
of every lonely man in town. No one
could say why it was her shoes were off,
or who the man holding her was. The sign
leaves him nameless, a ghost seen on nights

the Maumee threatens to rise with the moon and moan
through the streets, erasing names. The woman
I touched on the raw bones of that river
had many names. I only knew one. Her ghost
moans beside me down streets missing
their signs. On one, she gets up to feed her baby,
a man snoring his side of the bed to
some other town down river that mutters
curses at any lovers who lie and touch
in grasses thick along its body. Maybe

what moves through her into the child
is the sad river her husband dreams.
Maybe no matter how many times
she forgets herself, or returns to the lover
who longs to rub her feet of all soreness
and doubt, it's this river she needs
to pray to, to pray for, to ask weather
to keep it from rising, forgetting itself.
And maybe any longing is a dust
only a river swollen by weather

can wash off. Maybe all her names are prayers,
the faded white sign enough to forgive her
everything. Any river knows not to
lug a thing like guilt all the way to a gulf.
No matter how many names a river
picks up its length, it hums only one.
Until you break down and hold a river
all night, any name is just an excuse
for bitterness. To forgive yourself,
love every waitress and learn the foot.

Just Under What We Call Landscape

after Eva Lipman's Marc Ballroom Exhibition,
New York, New York. 1985.

> *Grace, like a scythe, cuts what it cradles.*
> —Eric Pankey

Light's the most versatile liar
of all. The possible angles
from light and dark and the awkward grace
of bodies raise doubts
about what's seen. Enough to believe
nothing's true. This blurred
man and woman dancing, in motion
licensed by haze and chemicals,
seem to whisper. Almost like the boy did

who fell into an abandoned mine.
His bruises sang operas
in languages he had never heard
or spoken. He must have imagined
the rope they threw him down
had been ripped out and lowered from
a sky so loud nothing could rise
out of his throat for weeks. The woman's
ankles are defined by light, almost

as though her feet are the only things
not moving, which can't be true.
The bodies have that haze
the sky can get over steaming water
near where sinkholes can take a house
in minutes, a woman undressing
for her lover the first time in the light,

drapes disappearing into dust
as the wall with her shadow caves in.

The angle of the sun etches silhouettes
of longing, almost prayers,
this couple's dance too formal.
The usual ache that collapses within us
with touch and raises a dust
we long to lick off a lover's skin
is held up by the oak timbers
of the dance. Tunnels that might trap us
are closed off with clear signs

even a curious boy couldn't ignore.
Bodies have no such signs.
For years, each time the boy touches
his lover he falls again,
and canaries yellow and drunk sing
with her moans. Light on naked bodies can
make truth give up everything
but touch. Severe silhouettes tell
various stories of awkwardness and grace.

One angle cuts the blurred figures
into a certainty not one of us
could put our faith in. Our bodies
are operas. On stage,
caged canaries sing music we'd claim,
but lies can only take us so far.
The curtain—red and stubborn
as a heart attack or the collapse
of tunnels long-dead miners carved

just under what we call landscape—
comes down and forgives the last note
still humming in our skin.
Forgives the audience—dancing awkward
in the aisles—for recalling
how everything collapsed around them
when a lover's body made the light
a fervent, whispered prayer,
the only lie they could live with.

A Hosanna for the True Curve of the Body

Holding on tight to beads of carved ash
scented with her fingers' sweat,
a woman recites foreign words
she wants to believe. The authenticity of
arthritis in her fingers cracks,
the harsh, marrow sound
the voice of regret the body's the seed of.

Pain needs no metaphor of nails in flesh
to convince her. Hanging in bodies,
it loves no one, and forgives
only the past—that crude crossbeam
from which memory sags,
a limp form to be eased down.

She tries to imagine her daughter's pain
is a stone to be rolled back
with enough faith, the beads burdened with
their token resemblance to
blurred images of light, the unnatural
curve of her daughter's cursed spine.

Even light has become her enemy.
Even this rosary witnesses
the shape pain carves with the body of
her daughter, each bead a vertabra twisted,
nailed to a torment of wood.

The memory of miracles entering
the world of flesh informs her
prayers for an angel to come
down and sing a hymn to the bone

in her daughter's spine, a hosanna
for the true curve of the body.

She's afraid angels don't remember flesh
clear enough to make music
that could bend a body right.
Still, she meditates on the mysteries,
each bead the solitary pain
of a saint whose suffering
is sign of a sick god's love.

Nothing's been said in rooms where light hums
through bones to give her reason
to believe her daughter's body
will heal, the spine a grimace.
She thinks of Christ brought down
from the cross, a contorted mime
of a man, bruised, bleeding,
not something the angels would sing of.

She touches the small cross and wants to
believe the god who made this
a sign of love understands her pain
enough to let angels sing
her daughter's spine into a cross
any man could be nailed to, and love.

The Burning Wheel Put Out by Its Own Turning

Behind the Ferris wheel,
in steel canisters
etched with what could have been

birds, hieroglyphics perhaps,
something decays.
The Ferris wheel is burning,

its flames making the birds seem
to dance, charred
and stoic. If steel canisters

can be marked with the carcasses
of birds, if a drunk
can find a niche to sleep in

and dream a Ferris wheel
lifts his mother into
a torn sky like a demented,

angelic ascension, then the burning
wheel can be put out
by its own turning. If

a camel moans and collapses
beside the drunk,
maybe he can heal it and ride

its withered hump to a city
he's heard of where
they build palapas for everyone

without a home. A camel,
he's heard, will
drill its hooves in mud to draw

maps with legends in hieroglyphs.
By the time the camel
is up, the Ferris wheel will be

full of strangers waiting to get off.
He will trust
the camel's direction. Saved from

the fire, his mother will hallucinate
a singed camel
pawing the figures of birds in mud.

WE CALL IT HOT BLOOD AND HUM IT

for Laetitia Casta

Fox squirrels are driving the common grays out,
the local news says. In a commercial,
pink ebbs down a stomach of clear plastic.
This is the way, folklore says, to a man's heart.
Not for Laetitia, the hottest woman in the world,
my friend says. Blood gives up the heart for women
like her. And the stomach, bloodless or not,
is just a cave with the best acoustics in the body.

Sometimes, the acoustic guitar a street musician
plays familiar ballads on for tips gets rained on
and swells into a kind of cave music dies in
without so much as an echo. I've seen it happen.
He coughed and apologized. No money was
enough. Later that night, I held a woman in bed
and scooted down to listen to her stomach.
Whatever was playing, it wasn't classical.

More like the slow frenzy of Monk on the piano.
Loss is, after all, a cliché. But you can't long
for what you have, though often we think
that is what we're doing. Thelonious knew
that song, a second set of ribs, was the hottest
music he could play. It's been too long
since I listened to that woman's stomach, loss,
at its best, a music no voice keeps up with.

It hums in the air, and the raw, gray hands
that were all Monk had left moved, rabid,
over the keys. The blood we hear in love,
we call it hot blood and hum it to ward off
loss. Even Laetitia will not be Laetitia
forever, beauty the first hint of loss we'd deny.
Jazz relies on this, music, no matter where
it comes from, the ache we can just bear.

DANCING IN MIAMI, OKLAHOMA

Old folks here say the sky
is a note held on a fiddle
longer than humanly possible.
They say they breathe bluegrass
in their sleep, a music
that makes the sky waver.
They have seen it tremble,
they say, and heard rain
hum melodies they swear they know

but can't name. One
old woman dances in
frayed cotton gowns every night
through the city park and home.
Boys grow up with the legend
of her withered flesh. Grandfathers
play old records at night
and swear her body once made
all of Oklahoma want

the sun to blind them just after
she left their sight. Fathers say
the one man who touched her
lives mad in a shack
alone at the edge of town,
where strays scrounge for scraps
and whimper at a sky
still out of whack
with the fiddle's music. Boys

throw rocks at the strays
and make fun of the lunatic
in the shack. History is
as much what people say
as what they do, and Oklahoma
is no more ground down
than any state. Dancers
under its callous sky
wouldn't be out of place flickering

across the tattered screen
in the theatre someone's been
restoring as long as the fathers
can remember. No one knows
what it was to begin with.
Teenagers drink and tell jokes
about the town's curves,
how the mayor's blocked efforts
to straighten Main. In his yard,

he watches an old woman dance
around the town's bend to a record
he breaks every night and buys
every day. His wife painted
baroque angels on the cornices
of the theatre and left.
Music can't restore anything
we lose. Grandfathers
can't swear to it, but believe

the old woman once played an angel
in a film where she restored a man
to his life. A Texas waltz
by Bob Wills helped her
into a gray sky at the end
of the movie. Everyone but the woman
goes to auctions. The rusted
farm equipment was theirs,
before the farms failed. No one

buys anything, but the auctioneer's voice
is a music of possibility
they want to believe. They want
to believe distance isn't everything,
and the rumor of touch
is enough to make strays forget
the note of the sky, enough
to bring gilded angels down
to save women who fall or dance

out of memories of falling.
Nothing, the mayor swears,
is actually straight. Everything is
at least a bit off. Old folks
don't care enough to argue.
They shut themselves in with old records
and whiskey to wait for
the lonesome night,
and a dancer they can count on.

SWING DANCING IN THE BLIND PIG

Ann Arbor, Michigan

Resurrected from a past
when a ghost drank and collapsed
against a pillar, or slipped
into what he must have believed
was a pew in a train station
open all night, this music
couples dance to could have,
in another state, another time,

roped and broke every horse
buried under the collapsed barn
that burned down. The man
who built it burned too,
ashes a boy sticks his fingers in
before he touches the terrifying mystery
of the girl's naked body.
It's not just the music,

which could be a soundtrack for a movie
the couples, dressed for a decade
they weren't alive for,
must believe is being filmed tonight.
It is that there's a ghost
who didn't pay to get in,
all his cash soot on the raw back
of some girl who wants music

to play and drown out the harsh dust
and hay drifting over her body.
Some things should be abandoned.

Ghost horses whinny in
the dust. The girl believes
she hears them. They make her feel
more than this filthy boy
pushing into her body

will bother to. The dead have
advantages over the living. Maybe
that's what nostalgia is: not
a longing for the past,
but for what the dead have
that we don't. Swing,
they call the music, and, when
they dance, it's a supplication

for what's been lost. Ask
the ghost sitting on the burned stumps
of his hands in a pew
in the boarded-up train station
if dancing with a woman
charred those hands, if
it was worth it. Horses snuffle
his poor legs, but his ghost hands,

if they do hold sugar,
are under some girl a boy's trying
to touch the way he's heard
it's done. He's drawn some figures
on her flesh in ash—a man,
a woman, and some horses
that burn inside her now,
where dry grasses could catch

and turn everything into ash
with nothing to say
about resurrection. Nothing
comes back but what's lost.
Swing, lovers, to music
that doesn't leave any ash
and comforts old horses
who nuzzle a ghost for love.

Hymns Not One of Us Would Risk

In northern Ohio, false pear trees hum like sleep,
swarms of bees between the almost-blossoms.
To walk under the deceptive trees, humming,
is like waking from walking in your sleep
on the whitewashed porch of a woman
who hummed when you made love, knowing
she's inside, in bed with another man, asleep.
Some escapes are bargains. Others blossom sore
within us no matter the season. In Oklahoma,
though, they say the sky is indifferent,
and loss hums its way into actual fruit and dies.

Rituals don't always lead to salvation. It seems,
though, something always has to die. A god,
or the heart of a man at least. Or Wild
Willy's, closed for years and boarded up,
spray-painted by drunk teens humming what hurt
their suddenly anonymous flesh. Figures
they sprayed crudely are exaggerated. Love
isn't what they're about. Tonight, a drunk forgets
the bar's been closed years and bangs on the door,
the *Open* sign lopsided, and cries himself home.

Tonight, orchards just out of town are hymns
not one of us would want to risk, Ohio
full of state routes dotted with stands where fruit
is sold right under the sky, nothing in it
but sweet absence. The drunks here are just
as forgetful, and stumble from bars humming
the same bluegrass. No one but a drunk
would sleep under false pear trees at the start
of summer, the trees humming down to him

of love. If bees, disturbed, drift down to sting him,
he'll wake with new pain and bless the dead.

THE OPTIONS OF MEMORY ARE NOT INFINITE

The motel south of town houses drunk ghosts
who rant. All they think of is flesh,
and so loss. One remembers a woman
in love with nasturtiums, and wants
to touch the drunk flowers all over
a woman in the motel's bar, not tattoos
but memory. Don't forget, she told him,
how sad fucking can be. Don't forget
how you buried me in flowers once

and sweated over my body for hours
before we watched, on TV, the local militia
give up and leave their compound,
confessing it had been a mistake,
the mistrust, their bodies bright with flowers
burned-in, one woman, naked,
a blistering field of nasturtiums.
The officer who covered her with a blanket
had scars on his hands that gleamed

in the harsh camera light, disguised
morse code. Almost out of the picture,
a man sat in front of an open truck,
garish art on easels and jewelry
flashing bruised in a crude sun. Flowers
cheap plastic around him, the glass
he drank from was cartoonish. Maybe
memory is morse code. *Dot:* music
in a motel room where bodies crack

and hum Elvis. *Dot:* cartoon animals
falling from clichés of Southwest rock
to flowers of dust, cringes of pure color.
Dot: ghosts stumbling through dust.
Dash: the pure hysteria of
a woman's body you believed
was prayer. *Dash:* the print of
a Japanese woman touching cloth
to quiet cynics with color. *Dash:* the calm

of flowers any lover could breathe in
without panic. *Dot:* the local militia
ranting dusty streets. *Dot:* a man
who hurls a woman against walls
for the clothes she wears. *Dot:* her
believing bruises are nasturtiums
blooming below her flesh. There is
no help. The options of memory
are not infinite, and cheap prints

in motel rooms are just lullabies.
The state route limps past town and curses
seasons the swamp rises. Ghosts
give up and forget flowers
and bourbon and loss. Love, she says,
hangs on motel walls tattooed, by headlights,
with the elongated forms of lovers.
Try to find, instead, a reproduction
of Utamaro's *Sewing*. Imagine

the woman's arms are nasturtiums
through the bruise of cloth,
the line she sights between her hands
the horizon. This is just
the left panel of an obscure triptych,
the woman's face a vague curse
of perfection. No motel room contains
Utamaro. The heart has to
live with being disappointed, or leave

for classier digs, for memory. The flowers
that cringe on her kimono
are nasturtiums. Furious, they incite militias
to burn themselves with flowers.
Bourbon, she said, tastes like a field
gone to bitter blossoms, the dead
left with dust and stale language. No ghost
is sober enough to argue. With memory,
nothing's set in stone. No one could

mistake the garish colors of a room
in this motel for a print by Utamaro,
where color is the pain he felt
for the loss of love in its object.
Break out the bourbon, she said.
The problem is we aren't nasturtiums,
and when we come back
we come back different. Try
naming every flower tattooed on

that woman in the bar who can't
remember her skin without color,
or which flower was first. No one
can get a thing out of the dead.
Across town tonight, she breathes
the furious scent of her husband's sweat
and comes. Garish art
can't make nasturtiums love,
or burn the heart into any flesh

with enough color to keep it from being
erased. To touch a tattooed lover
with Elvis singing low
is to mistake memory for the truth,
clichéd flowers for the longing
of the body. Nothing could be
more wrong. The code you believe
you've broken is too sad
and riddled with options to believe.

The Sleep of Wood in the Houses of Wrens

It's not the wrens but the girl in overalls,
his daughter, he talks to
cutting and sanding wood to build houses
wrens will only use if he doesn't
paint them. He used to paint them,
and they'd stay unvisited till they rotted
and fell into pieces she'd pick up

to save because it seemed something needed
to be saved. Nothing was. But
the splinter that festered in her finger
from one of the gray shards,
the one she didn't tell her father about
but pinched and pushed until she gave up
and let it rot its way into her blood,

that dead wood went dormant.
Sleep infected her years later
in another state where wrens
had so many houses built for them
they were transient, their song
a reminder everything just keeps going
and then is gone. Like that

shop thick with the refuse of wood,
like the garden with wrens singing Oklahoma
into a forgetful state where
a man who once drove a truck
could landscape his backyard into a paradise
hummingbirds and wrens and blue jays dance in.
When the heat was the worst,

they'd bathe in dry soil because
the council wouldn't let him water his garden
when it looked like there wouldn't be
enough water for people to drink in town.
Even the drunks, singing harsh,
took their whiskey straight, sacrifice
an angel that grapples with us

beside many rivers, even forgotten ones
that have gone to dust. Can we
expect wrens to live in graying wood and sing,
or a woman with gray wood
budding in her heart and other organs
to wake after only eight hours?
The sleep of wood is much longer

than the sleep of flesh. And wrens,
they sleep minutes at a time.
Building the houses, the man breathes in
dust from the sander and coughs.
The same dust clings in his daughter's hair
and makes her a woman
the most invisible wrens could live in.

THE PRECARIOUS RHETORIC OF ANGELS

Succulents can break the heart in deserts,
the way the man roped to an elm and burned
would have said he left his body
tied to that burning. No one remembers
what he'd done. For some, such haloed figures
wailing in the distance are mirages,
signs of the decay of angels that feeds soil
and makes their strawberries bitter.
That the man didn't die was a miracle.
Men who were there swear the flames just

went out, the charred flesh left with words,
a tortured syntax that made their ribs brittle.
Judgment, they say, sometimes comes in flames,
with signs sure enough to be read in flesh.
That man no one has the heart to touch, that fire
wouldn't have, whose tongue was seared dumb,
still growls at women, his charred mouth burning,
a language of longing and empty rhetoric.
The women have learned the vocabulary of
his grunts, and blush for past sins and dream

of blackened tongues turning their flesh to ash.
The women know the tongues of angels
are often dark. Angels know women sleep
between Heaven and the Fall. They swear
the voice they hear in dark bedrooms lit
only by the light of their translucent bodies
is God's. The man's lit flesh was a feeble light.
It was no one's fault, the mistake, and everyone's,
hate a bitter ash that drifts in the air of
ruined cathedrals that sing with wind. Maybe

it was the rope they bound him with that saved him,
words the men believed they saw on his body
the rope's last will and testament,
the rhetoric of the martyr. Sacrifice is
a mirage the heart would drink sand from and love
how its thirst was sated. What we believe
is almost never right, meaning too precarious
to depend on. The stone saints who'd tell us,
if they could, how wind burns their faces
have had their scars removed. The stone-cutter

pulled any arrows out and bound the wounds
and balanced the bodies on platforms
between the origin of praise and its objects.
Women are in love with the stone mouths
of saints. They imagine when the saints pray
they pray in the language of the jade.
They want their own prayers to live as long
without faith as it does without water.
Under the saints, they want to believe
there's enough water in the world to put out

everything that burns, to believe any soil
can produce strawberries sweet enough to heal
the most ashen mouth. The men who burned
the skin of the man made mute cower from
saints and the rhetoric of accusation. And jade
thrives even where soil's broken down,
a bitter garden, its color almost a dirge
in this town where guilt's an art people burn
into skin with colors that could be mixed
from ash. Elms lean toward town and implicate

everyone. Women cook elaborate meals
and leave them on his porch where something
needs to be chanted fervent enough to heal
mottled flesh. Ribs seem to be his favorite,
and the women make them so tender
stone tongues would shatter to praise them.
Strawberries they leave are never bitter. Miracles
can blind us enough to make us mistake
the heart for a comma in the grammar
angels use in cathedrals where the fallen

moan and hum the music of guilt. Envious
saints are just mirages of flesh in marble
or granite scarred enough. And angels praise
or extinguish flames, depending on their mood.
Not even saints guess right every time.
They enter deserts and speak to worn rocks
as if speaking to bones. Jade keeps them alive,
water stored up in thick leaves. Carved
for cathedrals, the jade covers their feet,
a stone lie of succulents that break off,

too delicate a detail for weather to ignore.
Bitter rain, leaning south with cold,
is a scalpel. So much nonsense has been written
to define what's been lost. Language can't
restore stone or glass or light. Not even angels
can speak words that could heal the flesh
of the man burned to an elm. His throat,
the women say, swirls with a smoke he coughs
drunk and stumbling through town, the music
of his charred lungs an accompaniment

for the dim, fluorescent hum of street lamps.
They believe stars are bodies that have
become burning, the tongues they speak in
precarious and orchestrated to confuse
a man's love for a woman with some myth
large enough for the sky. Saints have
to suffer in stone for a charred, broken man,
forgiveness a faint detail almost hidden
behind the hands of a saint reaching for
what could be strawberries, or bitter hearts

strung on a vine and pinned to an arbor.
The stone lattice could almost be the words
of a prayer in a language the angels
can't decipher, the stone-cutter's secret
praise for the woman he loved. So much
is easily burned in this world. Even cold
can burn flesh, or cringe jade leaves
into scarred and brittle tongues with nothing
to say about saints or lovers. And angels
long to enter women and burn themselves

into a seared language not even God
would understand, his memory of being
a man faded by now, his suffering
as dim as the sand dunes in a desert
lit by a quarter moon that could slice
stone berries like a sickle. North of town,
in an old cathedral opened by fire
to the wind and rain, a scarred man hums
in the rotten pews, his music rising
out of bitterness, blessing everyone.

George Looney's first book, *Animals Housed in the Pleasure of Flesh,* won the 1995 Bluestem Award and was published by Bluestem Press. His second, *Attendant Ghosts,* was published by Cleveland State University Press in 2000. In 2001, Pudding House Press published his *Greatest Hits 1990-2000.* His poetry has earned him a National Endowment for the Arts Creative Writing Fellowship, and two grants from the Ohio Arts Council. In 2003, poems of his won The Larry Levis Editors Award for Poetry from *The Missouri Review.* His poems and stories have recently appeared in such journals as *The Southern Review, The Kenyon Review, The New England Review, The Gettysburg Review, Alaska Quarterly Review, Ascent, Prairie Schooner, Hotel Amerika,* and many others. He is co-director of The Chautauqua Writers Festival, and serves as editor-in-chief of *Lake Effect* and translation editor of *Mid-American Review.* He is associate professor of English and creative writing at Penn State Erie, where he is program chair of a brand new B.F.A in creative writing he designed.

THE WHITE PINE PRESS POETRY PRIZE